The eye-catching zebra-striped cover of Osa Johnson's 1940 autobiography I Married Adventure continues to inspire readers and Johnson fans. Chanute, Kansas native Osa Johnson and her husband Martin spent decades documenting the native peoples, wildlife, and habitats of Africa, Borneo, and the South Pacific. Their films, photographs, and books are an invaluable record of our diverse cultural and natural world in the first half of the last century.

COWABUNGA SAFARIS
Africa under a rainbow.

Gary Clarke's
AFRICA

This is a

Limited Edition

of 1000 copies

of which

this is number

―――――――

Gary K. Clarke

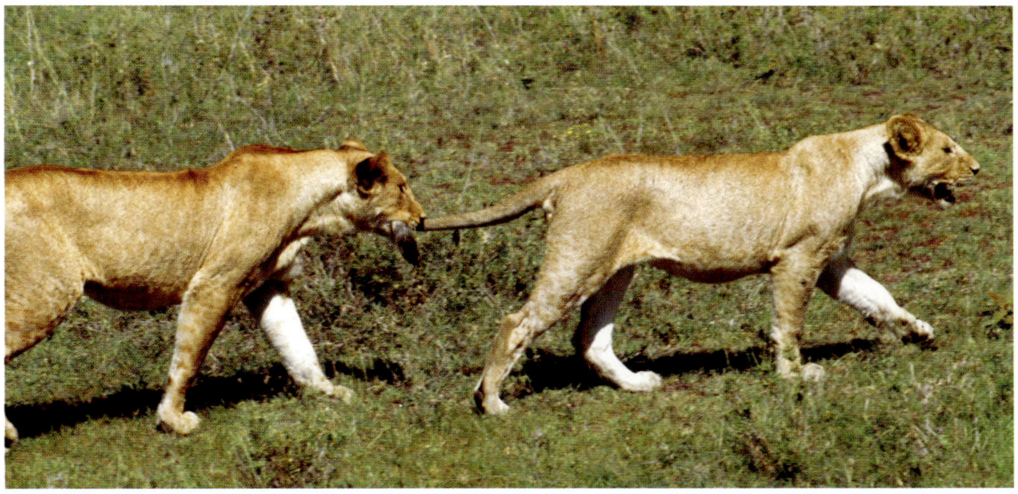

Books by Gary K. Clarke

❖

I'd Rather Be On Safari
Hey Mister—Your Alligator's Loose!
Gary Clarke's AFRICA: Wildlife, Rainbows and Laughter

❖

Forthcoming
They Call Me COWABUNGA! Once Upon a Time in Africa

❖

Words

With an oversized photo book such as this, there is a tendency to look at the pictures and not to read the text. The words in this book are few, but significant. They enable you to understand and appreciate the photographs.

—Jack Hanna
Director Emeritus of the Columbus Zoo and The Wilds
Host of Jack Hanna's Into the Wild and Wild Countdown

Gary Clarke's
A F R I C A

Wildlife, Rainbows and Laughter

If they cut out my heart when I die, I'm sure it will be in the shape of Africa.
—Gary K. Clarke

Gary Clarke's
AFRICA
Wildlife, Rainbows and Laughter

Photographic Essays Celebrating
Three Decades on Safari

◆

Gary K. Clarke, P.F.L.
Text and Photographs
(Except for photos that include me)

◆

Cowabunga Safaris (Pty.) Ltd.
Topeka   Nairobi   Johannesburg

© Copyright 2011 by Gary K. Clarke
Published in the United States by
Cowabunga Safaris, Private Bag 4863, Gage Center Station, Topeka, Kansas 66604.
www.cowabungasafaris.com
All rights reserved, including the right of reproduction in whole or in part in any form.
ISBN: 978-0-615-50180-2   Library of Congress Control Number: 2011910328

◈

Concept and Design: Gary K. Clarke
Digital Imaging: Joe Sutcliffe
Layout & Design Coordinator: Mary Napier, Napier Communications, Inc.
Editorial Advisor: Randy Austin
Technical Advisor: Sherry Best
Artistic Consultant: Rod Furgason
Book Development Consultant: Lloyd Zimmer
Production Coordinator: Jeff Taylor
End Papers and accompanying text courtesy of the
Martin and Osa Johnson Safari Museum, Chanute, KS

◈

First Edition
1 3 5 7 9 8 6 4 2
Printed and bound in the United States of America by
Jostens Commercial Printing, Topeka, Kansas 66609 USA

This book is dedicated—

To my family:
your love and support enabled me to follow my dream.

To my Cowabunga Safarists:
your camaraderie and commitment brought my dream to fruition.

To my African friends:
your acceptance and goodwill made me as one with you.

Contents

A Passion for Africa	14
Field Guide to an Endangered Species	18
The Bright Continent	23
The Fleeting and the Timeless	24
Images and Perceptions on Safari	
Awesome Africa	56
Natural Wonders of a Continent	
Bush Baby A-B-C's	66
Adorable, Beguiling, Captivating	
To Heaven in a Picnic Basket	78
Ballooning Over the Serengeti/Mara	
Wildlife Dignitaries	92
Unforgettable Animals (I Have Known)	
Skeleton Coast	108
Remote, Poetic, Silent	
Peoples, Traditions, Friendships	118
Cultures and Humanity in Africa	

Trunks, Tusks, Tails   136
On Being an Elephant

Hakuna Matata (No Problem)   148
*Life, Laughter and Unexpected
Eventualities on Safari—Just Now!*

To the Roof of Africa   174
Climbing Kilimanjaro at age 50

Let the Rest of the World Go By . . .   188
Zambezi River Canoeing and Camping

Would You Go on Safari with <u>This</u> Man?   202
Who the Cowabunga IS Gary Clarke?

Between Sunlight and Thunder   214
Quintessential Expressions of Africa

Visions of Africa   264

A Safari Prayer   266

Asante Sana/Ngiyabonga Kakhulu   268

Other Notions of Gary Clarke's AFRICA   270

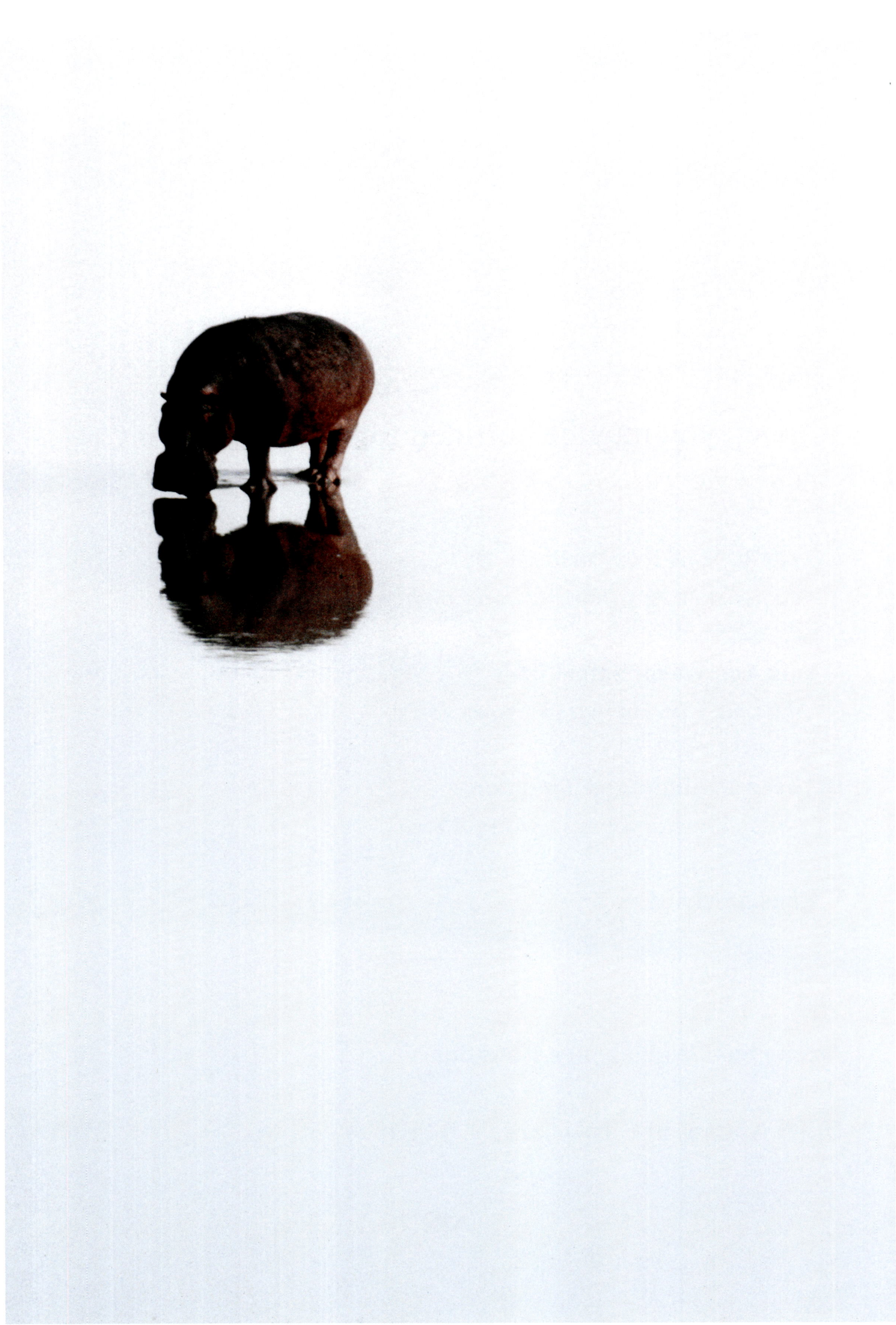

SAFARI

If you predicate the success of your
safari on one species (leopard, for example)
or on a single scenario (like a gorilla trek),
then you may be destined for disappointment.
But if you absorb all the wonders of
the bush—mammals, birds, reptiles, insects,
trees, plants, smells, sounds, spoor;
and if you live the adventure—
camping, exploring, trekking, climbing,
encountering cultures, canoeing, rafting,
ballooning, sharing, laughing;
and you embrace it all—
then you will be fulfilled
with a sense of awe
beyond every expectation.

—Gary K. Clarke

A Passion for Africa

Africa permeates my every fiber.

I was not born in Africa, yet I feel I am a son of Africa. For as long as I can remember I have had a mystical affinity for Africa—animals and cultures, geography and history—with an emphasis on wildlife. Nowhere on earth is there such an abundance and diversity of spots and stripes, hooves and claws, tusks and horns. And the contrasts: the swift and the ponderous, sunlight or darkness, heat or cold, dust or mud, life or death, a lone majestic elephant silhouetted against a blood red sky or endless migrations extending to the horizon.

AFRICA: a mosaic of wildlife, of habitats, of cultures, of humanity.

AFRICA: a term that has a myriad of connotations to countless people.

AFRICA: a term that stirs the imagination.

Within a week after I first set foot on the continent, the peoples of Africa filled my spirit, as did the sky and the wind, the rivers and the mountains, the deserts and the savannahs, and the incredible vistas.

So how did it come about—this appreciation for Africa, this fascination with wild animals, this passion to photograph it all?

It may seem curious, but from three dissimilar sources: a pair of zoos, a fictional character, and two very real people from Kansas.

The first zoo in question was the National Zoo in Washington, D.C., which during my childhood, inspired a lifelong empathy and rapport with exotic animals. The second zoo was the Kansas City Zoo, a magical place where everything I had read about animals came to life.

As you might imagine, the fictional character was Tarzan, and my first book in the series was a gift from my grandmother. Such adventure! I was hooked. To *live* in the wilds of Africa, to *commune* directly with those fantastic animals, *and* to sleep every night *in a tree*—WOW!

On a more realistic level was the daring young couple from Kansas (my birthplace) who pioneered photography in Africa: Martin and Osa Johnson. Such books as *Safari* by Martin and *Four Years in Paradise* by Osa motivated me to observe and to learn about animals, and to document them on film, while at the same time whetting my appetite for travel to Africa.

I soaked up Africa in every possible way: books, maps, films, lectures, museums, and zoos. In 1957, I began my zoo career in Kansas City, Missouri and subsequently became zoo director in Topeka, Kansas in 1963. In 1974, the Topeka Friends of the Zoo asked me to lead a photo safari to Kenya and Tanzania. I was ecstatic!

Thinking this trip would be my *one and only* chance to see Africa, I took hundreds of photographs, kept copious notes, made numerous acquaintances, developed lasting friendships, and absorbed memories sufficient for a lifetime. The memories and friendships have endured, but my initial safari was so successful that, thankfully, it became the first of many.

With each successive safari, I relinquished a fragment of my soul to the magnificent continent of Africa and returned home with the spirit of Africa beating in my heart. I admit that Africa seduced me. Nonetheless, I willingly succumbed. To me Africa was *not* a destination but a destiny, a raging passion, a fire within that was rekindled with each safari.

Even so, I would not have envisioned that climbing Mount Kilimanjaro in 1989 at age 50 would prompt a career transition from the dynamic world of zoos to life on safari full-time, sharing with others the majesty that is Africa.

For more than three decades (dating back to 1974), I was able to pursue this all-consuming fervor. On safari I would eat, sleep, drink, breathe, *live* all that is Africa. To observe the secret lives of incredible animals, to behold the cycles of the bush, to have rapport with the peoples of Africa—*and* to share all of this with others—was a special privilege.

My life and experiences in Africa have had a profound impact on me. As a person, I would be less than I am today if not for the overall gifts bestowed upon me by Africa: gifts of humility, insight, empathy, perspective, awe, joy, laughter, and friendship.

In return I can only hope that, in some small but positive ways, I have given back to Africa—to her peoples (especially to her children), to her wildlife, to her image and perception in the world. It is gratifying that my safaris over the years contributed economically to the tourism industry, creating employment and supporting many extended families, which hopefully developed an incentive to preserve wildlife and the environment.

Just as important, members of my Cowabunga Safaris groups have readily assisted Africa in so many respects: medical supplies for villagers; field equipment for anti-poaching rangers; camping gear for bush guides; specialty items for wildlife veterinarians; interpersonal relationships on social issues, and business ventures. And for the children?—*not* candy, but toothbrushes, ongoing financial support for schools, student supplies, books for libraries, magazine subscriptions, T-shirts, and soccer balls. These are but a few examples. The list goes on.

On their return to the USA, Cowabunga Safarists continued as goodwill ambassadors for Africa as they *realistically* shared their first-hand experiences through various discussions and programs. What an eye-opener for those in their audiences whose impressions of Africa had been formed primarily by Hollywood stereotypes and attention-getting international news sound bites.

I am at once extremely proud and tremendously grateful for *their* gifts to Africa: gifts of time and money, spirit and compassion. Long live the Cowabunga Safaris Alumni!

In developing a personal rapport with the peoples of Africa, my philosophy was to bridge any cultural gaps by simply expressing a bit of humanity. Sometimes the most satisfying gifts are intangible, yet heartfelt and sincere: a smile, a compliment, homage and civility to individuals, and respect for their African cultures, beliefs and lifestyles. Merely to speak to people in a bit of their local language is important, as it shows an appreciation for and a tribute to an individual's ethnicity, and always inspires a swell of pride.

Through my lectures, writings, and photographs, I have always endeavored to go beyond the world headlines and negativity about Africa, to clarify the persistent misconceptions, and to convey a more balanced and true feeling of the land, the wildlife and the peoples I love.

This book is a graphic interpretation of what Africa is to *me*. What a joy to share with you . . . my passion for Africa.

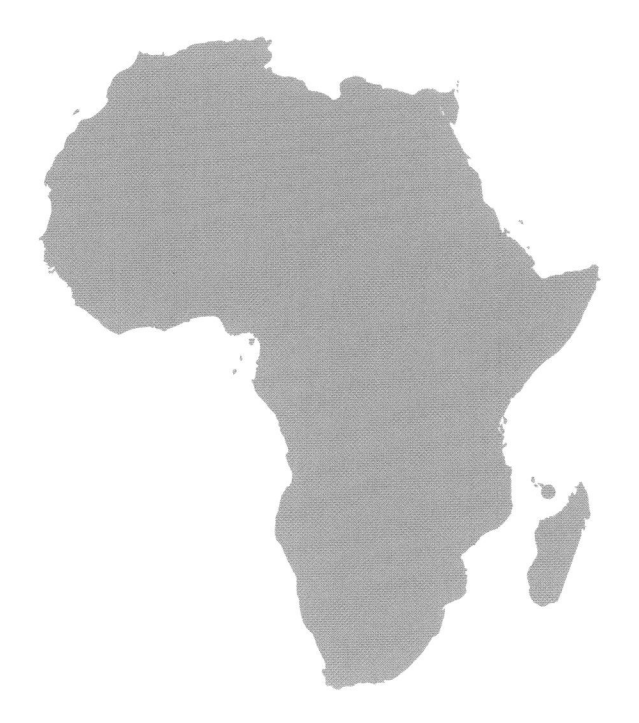

Field Guide to an Endangered Species

Please be advised, dear reader, that this book is an endangered species. I am not referring to some of the photos of rare animals *in* the book. What I am saying is that **this** book—in and of itself— **is an endangered species**.

Why? Because all the images were originally taken . . . on *film* (a somewhat outdated medium today). Most were 35mm color slides utilizing Kodachrome, Ektachrome, Agfachrome or Fujichrome. Some date back to the mid-1970s.

What this means for *you* is that the photographs in this book are all images "composed through the lens." They reflect the Africa I saw and felt at the time, with no embellishment or digital gimmicks. So, if there is a cheetah at the end of the rainbow, it is a *true* image and you will see it now just as I saw it then.

Real Africa. No tricks.

The reason that this book measures 10 inches by 14 inches is because a direct proportional enlargement of a 35mm slide equates *not* to 8 inches by 10 inches (the accepted norm), but to 8 inches by **_12 inches_**, and I did not want to crop my enlargements—I wanted to present them full-frame. Another reason for the size is that I find a photo that spans two pages annoying. The binding interval in the middle disrupts its aesthetic value (even if both sides match). Hence, *all* images in this book are flawless and uninterrupted, regardless of size. As a result, you will need to adjust your book one-quarter turn to properly view the horizontal images near the end of the book.

Let me begin by saying that I do *not* consider myself a photographer. I much admire those who truly qualify for the title. Many rightful photographers, both professional and advanced amateur, have been members of my Cowabunga Safaris groups. I have learned much from them. As for me, I have no formal training and possess only a rudimentary knowledge of cameras, lenses, filters, and other photographic paraphernalia. Consequently, I used a basic single-lens reflex camera, hand-held, with manual focus and manual film advance. My thumb often ached at the end of a long day. In later years, some pictures were taken with single use disposable cameras.

To compensate for this lack of photographic sophistication, I relied on my general sense of place in Africa, plus my awareness of animals and their anticipated behaviors (much of which I learned in zoos). For creative composition, I merely let Africa inspire me to see a familiar scene from a different perspective.

How I envied those elite wildlife photographers who could spend days, weeks, months—sometimes years—in Africa, devoting all their energies to shooting unlimited rolls of film to get "the perfect shot." I recognize that this "photographer's dream" is not as romantic as it might appear, and much admire their hard work, skill, and dedication. They have been an inspiration to me, and I salute their superb photos.

The pictures in this book are the result of what I call "field photography." By this I mean shooting pictures during a very busy safari itinerary in a group situation along with many other photographers—my guests. In my opinion, field photography on safari is the most difficult of all. You are under tremendous constraints: limited time, limited resources, and limited windows of opportunity. You are "shooting from the hip" and usually have but a single chance for that truly memorable picture. You must constantly be "at the ready" and the intensity of the moment can be nerve-racking as well as emotionally exhausting.

Photographing wildlife in Africa offers the supreme test. There are times on safari when—unexpectedly—all the elements for a photograph (or at least most of them) are present, often for just a few seconds or less. In that breathless instant you have to recognize that these conditions *do* exist. You have to be conscious of composition, aware of light and shadow, and, in the case of wild animals that are acting spontaneously, anticipate behavior! It is the ultimate challenge to photograph subjects in the wild under such conditions, yet the ultimate reward comes when the image composed in your mind's eye at that moment in time is preserved forever.

Throughout the book you will note that some of the captions are general, some are specific, and occasionally there is no caption at all (particularly at the very beginning and at the very end of the book). This is an intentional "reader participatory component." Now and then there will be just a bit of information about a photograph with the invitation "Your caption, please" for that picture. You are invited to be imaginative and to compose your own caption. I am most interested to see your captions, and would encourage you to send them along to me by snail mail. (See address on rear flap of the dust jacket.) I would also appreciate any other comments you have regarding the book.

Singular as Plural

In the old literature on African wildlife, it was customary to use the singular as plural for mammals (but not birds, reptiles, etc.). For example: "Four zebra were standing together" or "A pride of lion on a kill." I have imitated this style with the captions for this book as a tribute to those early writers.

Africa Far and Wide

The continent of Africa has more than 50 independent nations. At the end of each caption, I have listed the country of origin for each photograph. The map on the opposite page is provided as a quick reference for your convenience.

The Bright Continent

Depicted by early mapmakers as "the dark continent," I feel Africa is just the opposite—the bright continent: the bright sun and clarity of air, the bright colors of birds and flowers, the bright smiles of the people.

—Gary K. Clarke

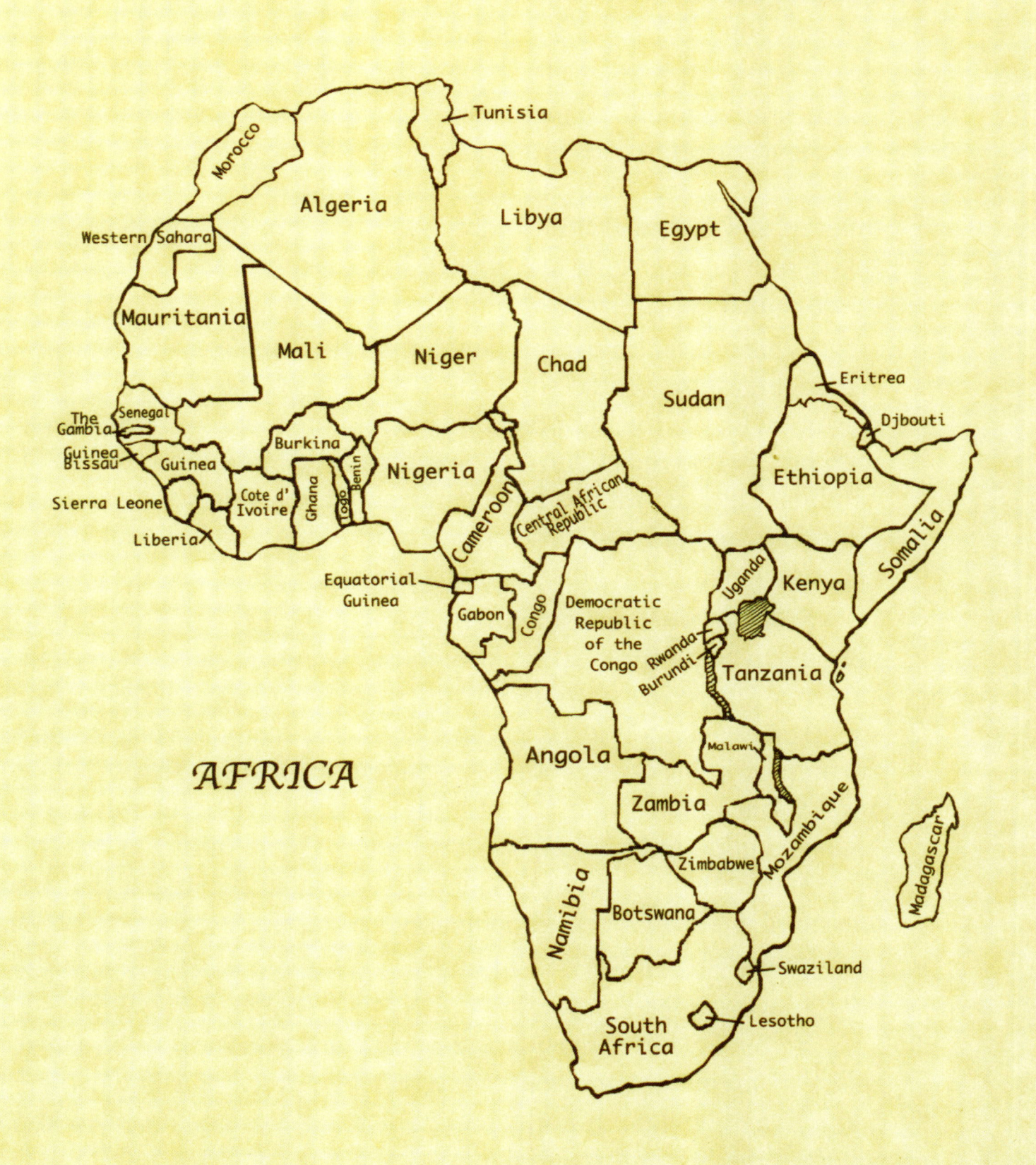

The Fleeting and the Timeless
Images and Perceptions on Safari

Africa is timeless. Its ancient rhythms pulsate within the oldest and most enduring land mass on earth. Yet the wildlife and natural qualities of Africa are fleeting. In the scheme of things, neither may last very long.

During the comparatively short span of my safaris (1974-2006), I witnessed dramatic change, both with the wildlife and with the safari experience itself. Africa is an exciting destination, but many of the adventures we had then cannot be duplicated today. In retrospect, I think of that period as the Golden Age of safaris. So, this book also serves as a record of those wonderful bygone days that too quickly became history.

What a thrill (and a privilege) it was to actually *be* there—in Africa, on safari—camera in hand. When I took these photographs it was not with the intent of creating a book. I wanted to share Africa with others, and did so through numerous slide programs and photo exhibits. The idea for this book came about years after the experiences portrayed, and only after the urging of my fellow safarists, as well as encouragement from others who had seen my photos.

Some of my most memorable moments on safari, however, were not preserved on film, particularly those that were the most intense (or "in tents") experiences. Not only does each tent zipper have a distinct sound, but each individual has an identifiable method when trying to zip and unzip in secret. Some use short spurts: "zip-zip-zip." Others employ one quick swish: "zzziiiiiiipp." I recall a particular group in which a budding romance was developing. One morning at breakfast I mentioned that last night I thought tent number two had a visit from tent number seven. Forks dropped onto plates and a couple of people asked in unison, "How do you know?" "Simple," I replied. "I could tell by your zip code."

If you have ever been on safari, not just with me, but on *any* safari—I invite you now to relax, with a cup of tea or a sundowner, and relive the magic. If not, then I hope to take you on an enchanting Safari of the Spirit, through the images and perceptions . . . of the fleeting and the timeless.

It was thrilling to me when my groups saw the distinctive feeding posture of the gerenuk. Kenya.

One field guide to African mammals described the elephant as: "Large, grey, unmistakable." Zimbabwe.

The skin color of a rhino indicates its habitat. This white rhino is brown from the soil. Kenya.

A mature bull elephant is dwarfed by the towering yellow fever trees of Ngorongoro Crater, Tanzania.

The Tarangire River serves as a vital ribbon of life for many species in the dry season. Tanzania.

Just below me, a lioness patiently observed potential prey from the cover of my vehicle. Tanzania.

Some say "J.A.I." (Just Another Impala), but I say impala are THE *quintessential antelope! Tanzania.*

Positioning its legs for balance, an elephant sleeps while standing, its limp trunk drooping. Zimbabwe.

Asleep on his feet, this huge bull rests his massive trunk on his right tusk (left tusk is broken off). Kenya.

This silverback mountain gorilla made arduous hours of trekking worthwhile. Rwanda.

A group of bull elephant socialize in the process of quenching their thirst. (Oh, I miss Africa!) Tanzania.

A pale (not albino) Thornicroft giraffe is one of 12 subspecies often recognized by taxonomists. Zambia.

In my experience a lion (or lioness) can look at *you,* past *you, or* through *you! Zimbabwe.*

Your caption, please. Kenya.

So confident in its arboreal abilities, a chimpanzee dangles over water knowing it cannot swim. Uganda.

The fierce sun casts deep shadows on a gemsbok (oryx) in its hard environment. Namibia.

Candelabra and yellow fever trees form Rift Valley décor for Cape buffalo and cattle egret. Kenya.

Indeed . . . the Safari tradition of hot tea and biscuits delivered to your tent at dawn! Botswana.

Meals were never more enjoyable than alfresco by the termite mound at our Zambezi camp. Zimbabwe.

Only after I saw this image in print did the title come to mind: Crocodile Tapestry. South Africa.

The sun sets on the Zambezi River in tribute to another well earned day on Safari. Zimbabwe.

A reticulated (with a net-like pattern) giraffe stands literally head and shoulders above all other animals. Kenya.

During mating, lions may copulate over 300 times in a week. The King of Beasts indeed! Tanzania.

Water is warmed by the campfire to the perfect temperature for bucket showers on Safari. Zimbabwe.

My friend Les suggested that I take this short-cut—obviously, the road less traveled! Uganda.

A bull elephant in the Zambezi valley stretches for the delectable pods of an apple-ring acacia. Zimbabwe.

Some people say elephant in the wild never stand on their hind legs . . . but I know they do. Zimbabwe.

To me, the appeal of this photo was not just the Grevy's zebra, but the lovely habitat setting. Kenya.

A statement of survival! The notched ear and scars (neck and hip) signify predator attacks. Namibia.

Sundown on Safari . . . the delight of living life as it is . . . . Tanzania.

The dramatic African sky and a lioness in the setting sun—the fleeting and the timeless. Zimbabwe.

Awesome Africa
Natural Wonders of a Continent

Africa is AWESOME!

So much so that, as a geographical entity, Africa is difficult to comprehend. I *love* Africa as a continent. I *know* Africa as a continent. I've studied the maps (old and new). I've traveled its remoteness and flown its length, as well as its breadth, non-stop (many times). I've seen photos of the continent taken from outer space, and yet—even for me—it is incomprehensible.

The dimensions of Africa are staggering. It is the second largest continent on the planet and makes up more than twenty percent of the earth's land surface. The confines of the continent would encompass the United States, India, Argentina, Europe, New Zealand . . . and China! To fly across Africa (west to east) from Dakar, Senegal on the Atlantic Ocean to Mombasa, Kenya on the Indian Ocean takes longer than to fly from New York to London.

Africa is AWESOME! The natural wonders of Africa include the world's longest river (the Nile: 4,160 miles); the world's largest desert (the Sahara: larger than the continental United States); and the world's highest mountain not part of a range (Kilimanjaro: 19,340 feet).

Many of Africa's wonders have been designated as World Heritage Sites. Foremost among these is Victoria Falls, which is twice as high as Niagara Falls and one and a half times as wide. It is the largest waterfall in the world by volume. To appreciate this fact, take a one gallon jug of water, pour it out and watch it "fall." Now visualize one hundred gallons of water . . . a thousand gallons . . . a million. Stay with me and visualize **140 million** gallons of water! That is how much water at flood stage flows over Victoria Falls—not in a year, not in a month, not in week, not in a day, not in an hour . . . but every minute! Yes! *One-hundred-and-forty-million-gallons* of water over Victoria Falls e-v-e-r-y m-i-n-u-t-e! In numerals, that's 140,000,000 gallons.

Without a doubt, Africa is awesome.

Over a mile wide, Victoria Falls is one of the seven natural wonders of the world. Zimbabwe/Zambia.

An awe-inspiring spectacle, Victoria Falls is known locally as Mosi-oa-Tunya, "the smoke that thunders." Zambia/Zimbabwe.

When the Zambezi river is in full spate, over 140 million gallons of water a minute roar 330 ft. onto the rocks below. Zimbabwe.

I took this unusual view of Danger Point in Zimbabwe from Knife Edge in Zambia. Victoria Falls.

At 17,058 ft., Mt. Kenya is the second highest in Africa. Early reports of snow near the equator were scoffed at by the geographers of the day. Kenya.

Extending over 4,000 miles, the Great Rift Valley has 30 active volcanoes. Tanzania.

Resembling a wedding cake, the 19,340 ft. snow-cap of Mt. Kilimanjaro can be seen from over 200 miles on a clear day. Tanzania.

Kilimanjaro is not only the highest mountain in Africa, but also the highest free-standing mountain in the world. View from Kenya.

The lovely Cape of Good Hope is often called "The fairest cape of all." South Africa.

Some consider rugged Cape Point (pictured here) to be the exact spot the cold Atlantic meets the warm Indian Ocean. Geographers, however, tell us that occurs to the east at Cape Agulhas, the southernmost point of Africa. South Africa.

A Cape fur seal colony resides on Duiker Island in Hout Bay south of Cape Town. South Africa.

Cape Town nestles at the base of Table Mountain and its tablecloth of clouds. South Africa.

The Ngorongoro Crater, with its varied habitats, is a microcosm of Africa. Tanzania.

Wildebeest and zebra are among the 40,000 large mammals that reside in this 102 square mile caldera. Tanzania.

Lovely Ngoitokitok Springs, on the floor of the Crater . . . soundtrack is hippo snorts and the cry of the fish eagle. Tanzania.

The balanced kopje rocks of Matobo Hills create one of Africa's most unusual landscapes. Kopje is pronounced "copy." Question: would a lion here be a kopje cat? Zimbabwe.

Bush Baby A-B-C's
Adorable, Beguiling, Captivating

Babies of any species seem to have a universal appeal—even baby warthogs and hippopotami—or maybe I should say *especially* baby warthogs and hippopotami. Cameras click and videos whirr on safari whenever we come across babies, accompanied by the predictable comments like, "Oh, it is (they are) so cute" and "I want to take it (them) home." I would often rejoin with, "What are you going to do with it when it grows up?"

While newly-hatched birds have little resemblance to their parents, most newborn mammals are a miniature of the adult. There are, of course, exceptions. Spotted hyenas are a pristine black at birth with the spotted pattern developing as they mature. In contrast, lions—a solid color as adults—have a spotted pattern as cubs that fades as they grow. Zebras have stripes at birth, and young zebras have what I call "brown baby fuzz stripes" that diminish with age. These examples (and many more) seem to be nature's way of helping the very young of some species to survive when they are most vulnerable.

One of the more fascinating survival behaviors between an animal parent and newborn is the "hider strategy" found in numerous African antelope species, such as the Thomson's gazelle. Prior to calving, the female will look for an isolated area with ground cover. If this is not available, she will deliver her offspring on open ground. The baby lies motionless and is nearly impossible to spot. (Once, while on a game drive in the Ngorongoro Crater in Tanzania, our alert and experienced driver slowed to a stop within one meter of a fawn in the open. We were astonished!) To reduce the chances of predators finding such calves, scent glands are inactive and the baby does not eliminate bodily wastes until stimulated by the mother's licking. The mother will periodically move her baby to a new location.

These are just the A-B-C's of bush babies; the D's through the Z's are equally as fascinating.

Giraffe at birth stand between 5½ and 6 feet tall and weigh from 110 to 150 pounds. Tanzania.

Your caption, please. Kenya.

The baboon mother's semi-erect tail helps balance baby on her rump. Tanzania.

While mother warthog kneels to graze, baby warthog kneels to nurse. Tanzania.

*Some say a black rhino baby always follows its mother.
This photo proves otherwise. Tanzania*

*Some say a white rhino baby always precedes its mother.
This photo proves otherwise. South Africa.*

Cheetah cubs have a mane of whitish hair, said to aid in camouflage . . . but I wonder. Kenya.

Your caption, please. Kenya.

The mothers of these sleeping orphaned rhino were killed by poachers for their horns. Zimbabwe.

Lion cubs remain in the security of the kopje rocks while their mothers are on the hunt. Tanzania.

Hippo may be born in water and can swim from birth. Kenya.

Young spotted hyena are such engaging creatures. The spotted pattern develops as they mature. Namibia.

The "brown baby fuzz" is apparent on this young plains zebra. Tanzania.

To Heaven in a Picnic Basket
Ballooning Over the Serengeti/Mara

A hot air balloon flight *anywhere* is magical, but a balloon flight in Africa is pure enchantment. I always cautioned my groups not to think of the flight as a game drive, even if they saw animals (that would be a bonus). Rather, think of it as a spiritual experience.

In my library of Africana (eleven-and-one-half-tons of books, periodicals, field guides, reports, safari journals, atlases, maps and various ephemera), I have an adventure novel entitled, *FIVE WEEKS IN A BALLOON*, or *Journeys and Discoveries in Africa by Three Englishmen*. It was published in 1869 by J. B. Lippincott Co. and the author is none other than Jules Verne, probably better known for his classic, *Twenty Thousand Leagues Under the Sea*.

At the beginning of *FIVE WEEKS* a publisher's note states that, while the geography of Africa as described is entirely accurate (based on the knowledge of the time), "The mode of locomotion is, of course, purely imaginary." Oh, how I wish Mr. Verne could have been in Africa with various Cowabunga Safari groups as we experienced, in reality, what he had only imagined.

We are exhilarated as we drift over the African savannah in a huge wicker gondola (holding 12 passengers) under an enormous, colorful envelope simply filled with hot air. The ascent is smooth and steady, and the flight is so unlike an airplane, floating rather than flying. Once aloft we see no super highways, no roofs of buildings, no parking lots, power lines or transmission towers—just pure Africa! We go where the winds take us. We marvel at the game trails, the rivers, the forests, the distant escarpment, *and* the vehicles of our chase crew so far below—bounding and careening over such impossible terrain that they seem like frenzied ants gone berserk.

Upon returning to earth we rejoice with champagne toasts (and I go off-duty), then a gourmet bush breakfast on the open savannah. It is all so dreamlike, beyond fiction. Even Jules Verne would be impressed.

An orphaned elephant responds to the gentle concern of visiting Cowabunga Safarists. Kenya.

To Heaven in a Picnic Basket
Ballooning Over the Serengeti/Mara

A hot air balloon flight *anywhere* is magical, but a balloon flight in Africa is pure enchantment. I always cautioned my groups not to think of the flight as a game drive, even if they saw animals (that would be a bonus). Rather, think of it as a spiritual experience.

In my library of Africana (eleven-and-one-half-tons of books, periodicals, field guides, reports, safari journals, atlases, maps and various ephemera), I have an adventure novel entitled, *FIVE WEEKS IN A BALLOON*, or *Journeys and Discoveries in Africa by Three Englishmen*. It was published in 1869 by J. B. Lippincott Co. and the author is none other than Jules Verne, probably better known for his classic, *Twenty Thousand Leagues Under the Sea*.

At the beginning of *FIVE WEEKS* a publisher's note states that, while the geography of Africa as described is entirely accurate (based on the knowledge of the time), "The mode of locomotion is, of course, purely imaginary." Oh, how I wish Mr. Verne could have been in Africa with various Cowabunga Safari groups as we experienced, in reality, what he had only imagined.

We are exhilarated as we drift over the African savannah in a huge wicker gondola (holding 12 passengers) under an enormous, colorful envelope simply filled with hot air. The ascent is smooth and steady, and the flight is so unlike an airplane, floating rather than flying. Once aloft we see no super highways, no roofs of buildings, no parking lots, power lines or transmission towers—just pure Africa! We go where the winds take us. We marvel at the game trails, the rivers, the forests, the distant escarpment, *and* the vehicles of our chase crew so far below—bounding and careening over such impossible terrain that they seem like frenzied ants gone berserk.

Upon returning to earth we rejoice with champagne toasts (and I go off-duty), then a gourmet bush breakfast on the open savannah. It is all so dreamlike, beyond fiction. Even Jules Verne would be impressed.

From the other balloon I had to calculate perfect timing to achieve this reflective image. Kenya.

A true "trial balloon" released in the chill dawn air to determine wind speed and direction. Kenya.

On their backs in the launch position (and unable to see what the noise was all about), I'm sure my groups wondered what I had gotten them into! Kenya.

After inflation by cold air fans, a huge tongue of flame dramatically blasts into the balloon envelope. Kenya.

*The noise of the burner and the heat from the flame
can be frightening . . . or reassuring—or both! Kenya.*

*The exhilarating ascent elicits a spontaneous
cheer of CO-WA-**BUN-GA**!!! Kenya.*

Vehicles and crew at the launch site quickly miniaturize as the balloon smoothly ascends. Kenya.

The rugged terrain below reminds you the balloon flight is by far the smoothest ride of your Safari. Kenya.

From the chase vehicle I anxiously photographed a male lion eyeing my Cowabunga group about to land. Kenya.

Once again the Cowabunga banner proudly flies over Africa. Kenya.

The breathtaking views of Africa from "the basket" offer some of the truly unique photo ops of the Safari. Kenya.

Many times I rode with the chase crew off-road through the bush on a bone-shattering, teeth-jarring pursuit of the balloon over unseen rocks, fallen branches, thorns, gullies, aardvark burrows, low termite mounds, hyena dens, skulls, and horns. Kenya.

While I advised my groups not to consider the balloon flight as a game-viewing activity <u>per se</u>, I also reminded them of the Cowabunga rule to always have cameras at the ready. Wildebeest and impala photographed from our balloon. Kenya.

When floating 'twixt heaven and earth over the savannah, Africa touches the soul. Kenya.

Just before assuming the crouched landing position, I snapped this photo of our ever-enlarging shadow as we descended. Tanzania.

A jubilant Cowabunga Safaris group upon landing in—? Somewhere in Africa.

The mark of a good balloon pilot is measured by his skill at popping champagne corks. Tanzania.

The hospitable balloon crews always brought EXTRA champagne for Cowabunga groups—asante! Kenya.

A celebratory toast from my groups was a signal for me to go off duty (just for a while). Kenya.

After the balloon flight, a bush breakfast on the Serengeti under the only tree for miles and designated by the balloon crew as Cowabunga Tree No. 1. Tanzania.

Wildlife Dignitaries
Unforgettable Animals (I Have Known)

Both as a Zoo Director and as a Safari Leader, the question most asked of me has been: "What is your favorite animal?" Many expect it to be a charismatic megavertebrate, or maybe one of the "Big Five."

The Big Five is a term often associated with the wildlife of Africa. It does not mean those animals that are actually the largest in size (neither the hippopotamus nor the giraffe is included). In fact the group even includes a species that seldom weighs over two hundred pounds. So, what *is* the Big Five? It is jargon for those animals considered by early big game hunters to be the most dangerous: elephant, rhino, Cape buffalo, lion, and leopard (the smallest).

To get a sighting and a picture on a modern day photo safari of each of the Big Five is an enjoyable goal (and deserving of a high five). Even more challenging is to achieve the same goal with the Little Five. These are smaller animals with names that include one of the Big Five: elephant <u>shrew</u>, rhino <u>beetle</u>, buffalo <u>weaver</u>, <u>ant</u> lion, and leopard <u>tortoise</u>. But the wonders of wildlife are more than the "Big Five syndrome." They are a true appreciation of all that nature has to offer.

To return to the question of my favorite animal: in all honesty the entire animal kingdom fills me with wonder and delight, but some of the most fascinating animals to me are the overlooked and the misunderstood.

It is so easy to make snap judgments about animals, or to assign them labels they do not deserve. I cringe when someone looks at a chameleon and says, "Oh, he is so *ugly*!" No, he is *not* ugly, especially to another chameleon. We use human standards to judge animal appearance, and that is unfair to the animal. Animals are not pretty or ugly, good or bad, nice or mean . . . they are as nature intended. They are not something we should try to make fit our gross misconceptions formed by cartoon characters or advertising gimmicks or other human measures.

As you view the animals in this chapter, accept them on *their* terms, not ours. Accept them for being the fascinating, wonderful creatures they are—accept them for just being themselves, alive in all their glory.

Chameleons, survivors from the dinosaur age, catch insects with a body-length tongue. Madagascar.

The grey crowned crane utters a haunting call in flight. Pairs perform an elaborate courtship dance. Uganda.

A bone-chewing giraffe! It is probably seeking calcium. Namibia.

After an encounter with an African crested porcupine, one warthog obviously got the point! Botswana.

A white-headed buffalo weaver collects nest material. Kenya.

The damaged shell (white spot, notch by leg) of this leopard tortoise may indicate a young lion has chewed on it. Tanzania.

I was lucky to photograph a silvery-cheeked hornbill deep in the forest, yet in good light. Tanzania.

Another lucky shot: a crowned hornbill as it caught a moth—just now. Kenya.

I have seen thousands of hippo in Africa, but very few rolling on their back! Tanzania.

The goliath heron may reach a height of 5 feet and feeds on frogs and fish. Kenya.

It is one thing to photograph flamingos when they are standing, preening, feeding . . . Tanzania.

. . . yet quite another to catch them on the wing (especially in poor light). Kenya.

The African wild dog is also called the Cape hunting dog (and sometimes the painted wolf). A social carnivore living in packs, it may be Africa's most efficient predator. South Africa.

The hyrax (or dassie) is quite common on top of Table Mountain. South Africa.

Preferring open savanna, the secretary bird hunts snakes, lizards and rodents. Kenya.

*I've often thought that the marabou stork might be called the "paradox" bird.
When gracefully soaring at high altitudes, people say it is lovely.
When standing close and personal, people say it is ugly. Rwanda.*

I've often thought that the warthog might be called the "paradox" mammal. When trotting along with its tail in the air, people say it is adorable. When kneeling close and personal, people say it is horrible. Tanzania.

Female saddle-billed storks eyes are yellow, males dark brown. Which sex is this one? Zambia.

The Nile monitor is a large and powerful semi-aquatic lizard. Botswana. (I sometimes told my groups to be sure to monitor this lizard.)

A mature male Cape buffalo, caked with mud—a true "Old Dagga Boy." Tanzania.

SEE YOU ON SAFARI—BILL YOU LATER. Shoebill or whale-headed stork. Uganda.

Skeleton Coast
Remote, Poetic, Silent

Africa is a cold continent with a hot sun, and this is particularly true in the desert. Remote and unforgiving, Africa's deserts are lands of wind and sand, beauty and majesty; lands of myth and mirage, silence and solitude. At the margins of the known world, the formidable deserts of Africa reveal the spiritual heritage of the continent.

The Sahara, sometimes called a vast expanse of mesmerizing desolation, is the largest desert on earth. It stretches for 3,700 miles between the Red Sea and the Atlantic Ocean and measures 1,200 miles from north to south. The Kalahari, with its diversity of landscapes, is a journey to a lost world and covers half a million square miles. And the Namib, the oldest of deserts, dates back three to four million years. Where the hot desert sands meet the cold ocean currents, the Namib covers a distance of 1,250 miles along the Atlantic coast of Namibia and extends 30 to 90 miles inland.

A remarkable feature of the Namib is the Skeleton Coast, a barren and inhospitable wasteland so named because of the many skeletons of rusted shipwrecks and bleached whale bones scattered along the mist-enshrouded beaches. It is the epitome of wilderness, with an aura of the distant past, an aura of mystery and tranquility.

On safari, particularly in the desert, I advised my groups to "always expect the unexpected." This was a set-up, but they had no clue. After a long day bouncing over rugged terrain everyone would be ready to return to camp, which they knew was some distance away. At dusk, under the descending cloak of a night chill, spirits would sink with the rapidly setting sun. Then, just over a sand dune and in the near darkness, a scene so enchanting it seemed a mirage: a welcoming campfire casting dancing light and shadows on a well-stocked bar, circled by chairs, complete with elaborate hors d'oeuvres and graced by the Cowabunga banner! With such magical sundowners on the Skeleton Coast, any thoughts of returning to camp were quickly dispelled. What fun . . . what memories . . . .

The Namib, a land of wind and sun, of mystery and tranquility. Namibia.

A skull and crossbones on the airstrip windsock—how appropriate. Namibia.

Eye-catching patterns are formed by light and shadow in the Namib. Namibia.

Our Land Rover . . . miniscule in the vastness of the Namib. Namibia.

Gazelle-like springbok antelope can survive on desert vegetation and its residual moisture. Namibia.

On the Atlantic coastline, where the desert meets the ocean. Namibia.

Often called living fossils, many Welwitschia plants are over 1,000 years old. Namibia.

Cresting a dune sculpted by the wind. Namibia.

The immensity and the splendor of the Namib desert are profound. Namibia.

Hot tea to your tent at sunrise helps ward off the desert morning chill. Namibia.

The secrets of the desert beckoned to us daily. Namibia.

We pause by a whale skull while braving the frigid, blustery wind off the Atlantic Ocean. Namibia.

Wind, sand and sun, together with the skull and jawbone of an oryx, are emblematic of the Skeleton Coast. Namibia.

Footprints in the sands of time? Or oryx tracks? Namibia.

Peoples, Traditions, Friendships
Cultures and Humanity in Africa

Africa, though a short single word, is a web of endless complexity in its political and cultural structures. There are more than 50 nations on the continent, each with its own history, traditions, religions, cultures, ethnic groups and languages (which make Africa all the more interesting). As safarists we would be guests in many of these lands. My groups needed to be mindful and appreciative of indigenous cultures and local lifestyles, to *not* expect things to be like the USA.

INSTANT AMERICA versus PATIENT AFRICA was a heading I used as part of my safari briefings. In the USA, we live in an instant society: the internet, cell phones, digital photos, fast food, ATM money—even instant nature on television. We quickly grow impatient when we have to wait. Africa is on a more natural pace. Waiting is a part of everyday life. Most Africans are patient, respectful, soft-spoken, and self-reliant. Cowabunga groups were quick to adopt these qualities in return, and invariably their interactions with the peoples of Africa were replete with mutual respect and genuine friendship.

The success of my safaris was attributed to how well my groups were looked after by my African friends: drivers, guides, trackers, rangers, naturalists, bush and balloon pilots, together with camp managers, cooks, waiters, barmen, receptionists, housekeepers, porters, chase crews and many other quiet heroes—*all* of whom were key members of the Cowabunga Safaris Team in Africa. I am forever grateful to these wonderful people. I fondly recall *their* smiles as we would sing the "Cowabunga Chorus" to them. I recall their singing, in return—as well as their dancing, ceremonies, special cakes, gifts, and surprises. I miss them and treasure their friendships.

I so enjoyed joking with the Africans, especially the various camp staffs. In the mornings, as I emerged from my tent, they would politely inquire, "Cowabunga—how did you sleep?" I would reply, "Lonely" and they'd quickly respond, "Oh, Cowabunga! We'll take care of that *tonight*!" Emphatically I had to tell them that I was **only joking**.

A Samburu dancer at the height of his jump. Kenya.

A Kikuyu Chief plucks his whiskers while contemplating responsibilities. Kenya.

Goatskin on this Himba woman's head indicates she is married. Each plait of her braided hair is wrapped in ochre clay. Namibia.

At the "Singing Wells" near Marsabit, people chant as they rhythmically dip, heave upward and dump heavy buckets of water. Kenya.

Samburu warriors in ceremonial dress. Kenya.

The Mikishi create elaborate masks. Zimbabwe.

Maasai wearing ostrich feathers (left) and a lion's mane (center). Kenya

In westernized dress, a young mother and her baby visit a rural medical clinic. Zimbabwe.

A little girl in traditional dress sells dolls made by her mother. Kenya. (Yes, of course, I bought one.)

With permission, I took this photo of a Maasai woman on my second Safari in 1975. Kenya.

What better classroom than natural Africa herself? Zimbabwe.

After delivering supplies to a Maasai school, I show the students my magic thumb. Kenya

Visiting, playing and laughing with children—Africa's most precious resource. Zambia.

As we depart in a boat from their fishing village, children rush to show me their magic thumbs. Zambia.

The conical tower in the Great Zimbabwe ruins—an ancient stone city that flourished from the 12th to the 14th century. Zimbabwe.

The Jomo Kenyatta Conference Center tower in Nairobi—a contemporary African capital city that is flourishing in the 21st century. Kenya.

I was struck by the artistic expression of this carved door. Zanzibar.

Oohhh . . . I've got a lovely bunch of coconuts! (Sorry about that, but what did you expect?) Zanzibar.

The City Market in Nairobi, Kenya.

Eggspression! Kenya.

Olla! A plethora of popular pots. Kenya.

A few of the many important members of the Cowabunga Safaris Team in Africa. Kenya.

Drums and singing welcomed my arrival by boat at Chiawa Camp on the Zambezi. Zambia.

My Botswana friends find mirth in my T-shirt which reads: "bald head" and "big belly." Botswana.

The ladies of Susi and Chuma Camp always had smiles and sundowners-at-the-ready. Zimbabwe.

A lively Equator crossing adjacent to a curio shop is typical of today's Africa. Kenya.

A quiet Equator crossing by a family's banana trees is reminiscent of yesterday's Africa. Uganda.

Friendship is an unexpected cold beer when passing through a balloon pilot's camp. Kenya.

Friendship is an unexpected shower of gifts (cashews, tea, liquor) at the end of a Safari. Tanzania.

Crowded Africa: Passengers disembark from an overflowing ferry in urban Banjul, Gambia.

Uncrowded Africa: A camel caravan traverses the remote Northern Frontier District. Kenya.

Trunks, Tusks, Tails
On Being an Elephant

Elephants may very well be the most compelling symbol of the animal kingdom. Familiar to everyone, elephants hold a great fascination due to their enormous size, unique appearance, and three distinguishing characteristics: trunks, tusks, and tails.

More than a prolonged snout, an elephant's trunk is a double-tubed proboscis that serves as its lifeline to the world. The trunk is a nose with nostrils at the end, and elephants breathe through it. They lift it high in the air to enhance their keen sense of smell, and gently touch things with it to get a scent *and* a "feel" of the object. Let an elephant encompass your face with the end of its trunk (usually dripping with mucus), and you gain a better understanding and appreciation of this amazing appendage; and when they blow in your ear . . . well . . . .

To drink, they suck water (three to five gallons at a time) part way up the trunk and blow it into their mouth. To eat, they curl the end of the trunk around the food item, or pick it up with the two "fingers" at the tip, and place it in their mouth. Zoologists agree that the trunk contains at least 40,000 muscles.

Tusks are modified upper incisor teeth and are larger in males. They are used for protection, to dig for water and minerals, and to strip bark off trees. Elephants have only four functional teeth at a time: one large, deep-set molar in each jaw—upper and lower, left and right. They have six sets of these teeth during their life. Elephants can live well into their fifties.

The tails of elephants can indicate their emotional state, while the "tales" of elephants can arouse our emotional state.

That elephants are hard to describe is evidenced by a reference in a prominent field guide to African mammals that states, "Elephant: large, grey, unmistakable." The African bush elephant is the largest living land animal. Adult males may stand twelve feet at the shoulder and weigh more than 12,0000 pounds.

Lions may be the king of beasts, but elephants are lord of the bush.

The trunk of an elephant has over 40,000 muscles, and serves as its lifeline to the world. Zimbabwe.

Male (or bull) elephant often associate in groups with a complex social hierarchy. Tanzania.

Elephant families are matriarchal, with the oldest female (or cow) serving as the leader for her daughters and granddaughters, as well as for other female kin and for juveniles of both sexes. The female in the center is giving chase to some wildebeest. Kenya.

After many hours of waiting and watching in an underground hide, I was rewarded when a group of elephant came to drink and play at the waterhole. Zimbabwe.

Adult elephant protect youngsters by keeping them within the herd. Zimbabwe.

The trunk is not a straw: elephant drink with *it, not through it. Zimbabwe.*

When drinking, water usually drips from an elephant's mouth. Zimbabwe.

After quenching their thirst, elephant enjoy playing in the waterhole. Zimbabwe.

What a thrill! From the bunker, I was so close I could have touched their legs (I didn't). Zimbabwe.

Dampness inside the hind legs indicates this solitary bull is in musth, a breeding condition. Kenya.

Even adult elephant like to play in the mud. Zimbabwe.

This makes me want to be an elephant—or at least play in mud! Zimbabwe.

*Your caption, please.
Zimbabwe.*

Mud. **Glorious mud!**
Zimbabwe.

*Your caption, please.
Zimbabwe.*

The skin of an elephant, when wet, turns dark and shiny. COWABUNGA! Zimbabwe.

When this elephant charged, only my shutter finger moved . . . and maybe my bowels . . . . Zimbabwe.

Hakuna Matata (No Problem)
Life, Laughter and Unexpected Eventualities on Safari—Just Now!

Africans have told me that Cowabunga Safarists are "a force to be reckoned with" due to their enthusiasm for Africa, their zest for life, and their willingness to do what other groups would not consider.

Imagine the audacity of my taking ordinary and unpretentious people to the wilds of Africa and having them experience the most unexpected and ridiculous of scenarios, like: tracking *black* rhinos on foot; eating mopane worms for snacks; climbing into the hollow cavity of an enormous baobab tree; competing in a wildebeest "dung spitting" contest; sliding on their bottoms down the highest sand dunes in the world; and wallowing in mud churned by elephants and buffalo.

YES! Cowabunga Safarists were eager participants in all of these delights. They showed their true mettle, their spirit of adventure, and how the safari experience is much more than wildlife sightings and photography. I am so proud of them! Ranging in age from pre-teens to octogenarians, they embraced the Cowabunga Safaris philosophy to the *nth* degree. Safaris can be serious, but they can also be so silly. How wonderful to see people, regardless of age, behaving and laughing with the abandon of carefree children.

Cowabunga Safarists have a common bond that brings a spiritual quality to the group as they share unique adventures together. They learn the true meaning of "T.A.B." (That's Africa, Baby) and *Kundi Bora* (Kiswahili for "the best group"). Instead of saying, "so far, so good," they say "Safari So Good," and they vigorously sing the Cowabunga Chorus. It is gratifying to me each year when I receive holiday cards from people who went on just *one* safari, some as long as thirty years ago, and yet they still speak of the laughter.

Here is a classic photo of one Cowabunga Safaris group in a hole in the trunk of a huge baobab tree. It also shows where the elephants, with their tusks, have stripped the bark off. The elephants mistook the baobab for an acacia, so they were . . . barking up the wrong tree.

My group in a baobab tree answers the question, "Who has more fun than COWABUNGA?" Zimbabwe.

Enthusiastic Cowabunga, not knowing what the bush may bring, but ready! Zimbabwe.

The obligatory group photo on Safari, complete with a license plate from my Jeep. "Biltong" is the African term for what we Kansans call jerky, and many of my outdated plates proudly hang in the bars of various camps throughout Africa. Zambia.

In the middle of Ol Kokwa island in the middle of Lake Baringo in the middle of the Great Rift Valley in the middle of Africa, helmeted guineafowl and a female waterbuck sometimes show up for afternoon tea. (There is no *window.) Kenya.*

I should have known better than to ask my group to show me where we were on the map! Somewhere in Africa.

Your caption, please. Uganda.

It is even more exciting to cross this river at night amid reflected eyes of hippo and crocodiles. Kenya.

Come hell or high water, Cowabunga carries on . . . . Kenya.

Your caption, please. Zimbabwe.

No seat belts, no roll bar—these are true Cowabunga Safaris adventurers! (I walked down.) Zimbabwe.

Dozens of photos of thousands of flamingos in the Great Rift Valley. Kenya.

Eeiii! The water is COLD for the Cowabunga ladies in the Okavango Delta! (Beware of leeches.) Botswana.

Cowabunga Safarists really know their . . . . Tanzania.

Your move, please. Tanzania

Elephant have right of way, as well as hippo. Zambia.

All of Africa knows Cowabunga Safaris by the sign "Kundi Bora"—the best group! While it is certainly exciting to be among the elephants in an enclosed van . . . Kenya.

. . . it is a real adrenalin rush in an open vehicle! Zimbabwe.

OK, Cowabunga ladies: credit cards at the ready . . .

. . . for a shopping frenzy on Safari! Kenya.

A photo of me taken from outside the Cowabunga baobab tree . . .

*. . . and the photo I took from inside the same tree
(note the rainbow on the horizon). Tanzania.*

The morning after!
Empty Tusker beer bottles memorialize the intensity of sundowners the night before. Kenya.

*Cowabunga rule number one: <u>Always</u> have emergency toilet paper for the bush loo
(ladies behind the baobab tree, gentlemen behind the termite mound). Somewhere in Africa.*

Few things are as satisfying as marking your territory in the bush. Whereever in Africa.

One of my favorite "T.A.B." signs (That's Africa, Baby). Zimbabwe.

Cowabunga Safarists warming their buns in "Coldest Africa." Zimbabwe.

Your caption, please. Somewhere in Africa.

The traditional "Cowabunga Greeting" by a termite mound along the Zambezi. Zimbabwe.

On Safari you can act silly and no one will say, "Oh, why-don't-you-grow-up?" Zimbabwe.

The Victoria Falls Hotel doorman proudly displays his badge from the World Famous Topeka Zoo. Zimbabwe.

Hyena dung is white (from calcium) and used as chalk in remote Africa. Zimbabwe.

The Safari Life: On the trail at sunrise, a picnic lunch at midday, sundowners in the bush, and then continue after dark with a spotlight in search of elusive nocturnal animals. **Ne plus ultra!** *Zimbabwe.*

Frequently my groups would show blatant disrespect for the Cowabunga Safaris banner . . .

*. . . soooo . . . **payback time!** (At long last!) Zimbabwe.*

Your caption, please. Somewhere in Africa.

To the Roof of Africa
Climbing Kilimanjaro at age 50

It was like I had just half a lung, like I had a plastic bag covering my face, like my boot laces were tied together.

That was how I felt in the final agonizing hours as I struggled toward the summit of the highest mountain in Africa. Climbing Kilimanjaro was simultaneously the most glorious—as well as the most horrendous—adventure of my life.

I am not a mountain climber. I'm not even athletically inclined. So why even *think* of such an absurd endeavor? Certainly not for the oft stated, ". . . because it is there." No. I had a more compelling reason, one that called from deep within my psyche. From the moment I first saw Kilimanjaro with its massive, snow-covered summit high above the clouds, seemingly disjointed from the earth and suspended from the heavens, I knew that someday I must stand on the pinnacle of that magnificent continent—on the roof of Africa.

The base of Kilimanjaro is 37 miles long by 25 miles wide. When climbing it one experiences seven life zones—like traveling from the equator to the Arctic. On many safaris, I lived in the shadow of Kilimanjaro. I was awed by its commanding presence and saw its many moods. I had completely circled it by air and flown directly over the Inner Crater of Kibo, the highest peak.

Kilimanjaro beckoned.

The first documented ascent was by Hans Meyer in 1889. After training for two years, I climbed it in 1989, while celebrating my 50th birthday. During the climb, I consumed 4,000 calories a day, yet lost twelve pounds in six days. On the descent, I was so exhausted that the head guide called the rescue team to help me down. My goal was not to conquer a mountain, but to realize a dream. I did, and in doing so, I conquered myself. I came back from Kilimanjaro a changed man.

Whenever I see Kilimanjaro (or even a photo of it), it is hard to believe I was really up there. But my aching body tells me it is true. Actually, I climbed Kilimanjaro *twice*: the first and the last time.

My first sighting of Kilimanjaro in 1974 filled me with emotion and inspiration. View from Kenya.

The highest peak of Mt. Kilimanjaro (Kibo) seems to float in the African sky above the Momella Lakes, with an island of candelabra trees in the foreground. Tanzania.

After two years of training, I began my climb a few days before my 50th birthday in January 1989. Tanzania.

We started in montane rain forest, with dense vegetation and exposed tree roots. Our porters balanced heavy loads of provisions on their heads. Tanzania.

Unseasonably heavy rains in some areas made the trail a sea of mud. Tanzania.

Giant senecios and lobelias gave an "other-world" atmosphere to the heather/moorland region. At times we were climbing in ankle deep water. Tanzania.

Grim misgivings swept over me at the last water point . . . the most difficult part of the climb was still ahead, and our only water would be what we could carry from here. Tanzania.

Often the trail was strewn with ankle-twisting rocks and concealed holes that made treacherous footing. Tanzania.

While crossing The Saddle, a barren desert between Mawenzi and Kibo peaks, I experienced intense sun, then rain, then hail, then wind, then bitter cold—with no shelter! Tanzania.

Much of the time I could not see Kibo, (a psychological downer, as reaching Kibo was our goal). Our spirits soared when it was in sight, especially in sunshine. Usually, though, it was overcast. Tanzania.

Pausing to catch my breath, I looked back at Mawenzi, the second highest peak on Kilimanjaro. By now oxygen was half that of sea level, and as a result I was truly suffering. Tanzania.

The night prior to our final ascent, I could not sleep: too tired, too cold, and had to urinate every 30 minutes (or at least it felt like I had to, which is just as bad).

A little before midnight our guides roused us for a cup of hot tea and a biscuit. We departed at 1:00 a.m. Several hours later we reached Hans Meyer Cave at 16,737 ft., where I collapsed on a pile of jagged rocks.

While lying there, gasping for air, I noticed two climbers silhouetted at the Cave entrance. It was such a wonderful image that I mustered enough wherewithal to get the shot. Tanzania.

Proceeding onward from the Cave, the unending switchbacks in the deep snow were dreadful. My just-turned 50 year old body was far beyond its physical capabilities, and each labored step was by sheer determination.

Two climbers from other groups had died during our time on the mountain. My thoughts now returned to a few days earlier, when we watched in silence as the body of one of them was carried down past us.

It was not that I wanted to die. But as bad as I felt at this point—I didn't care if I did. Tanzania.

On reaching the summit, I was impressed with the large glaciers on the edge of the crater. Tanzania.

The guides were thrilled that "Cowabunga" had climbed to the top of Kilimanjaro at Gillman's Point, with an altitude of 18,635 ft. The very highest spot on the summit is Uhuru Peak at 19,340 ft. However, the trail was closed due to deep snow. Just as well; I didn't have the energy. Tanzania.

From the top of Kibo I looked down on Mawenzi, Kilimanjaro's second highest peak at 16,893 ft. I've always thought this photo looks as if I had taken it from an airplane. Tanzania.

An African fish eagle and a classic acacia tree accentuate the Snows of Kilimanjaro. Tanzania.

Let the Rest of the World Go By . . .
Zambezi River Canoeing and Camping

"What's your favorite place in Africa?"

A fair question, and one that is nearly impossible for me to answer. Let's see: Serengeti, Kalahari, Okavango, Kilimanjaro, Ngorongoro, Etosha, Zanzibar, Timbuktu—how can I choose? These are just a few locales, and I do not consider one better than the other. They are all so different, and each is special in its own right. To be candid, as long as I was on safari, I was happy wherever I was in Africa.

But, if I could return to Africa just one more time, I would go to the Zambezi, canoeing down that marvelous river wearing my T-shirt that reads: *Love many, trust few; learn to paddle your own canoe.*

Never does one feel so infinitesimal, so inadequate as when the bow of your puny canoe quietly anchors at the edge of an island in the Zambezi, with the most magnificent of bull elephants towering above you, his back seemingly touching the heavens!

It was always such fun on canoeing safaris to surprise groups with lunch at the "best restaurant on the Zambezi" (a picnic *in* the river while sitting on small stools, ankle-deep in water on a sandbar), and to camp overnight on an island *without* tents, just sleeping bags. In their travels, many of my safarists had stayed in five-star hotels. But while lying in the sand on an island in the Zambezi, looking at the sky, they knew they were in a *million-star hotel*, and that friends back home would never believe it.

When people learn that I led safaris, one of their first questions is: "Did you have any close calls?" The answer is usually disappointing, as there have been surprisingly few. The one incident that does come to mind occurred while canoeing on the Zambezi. My partner was paddling in the back and I was in the front to take photos, intently concentrating on a beautiful kingfisher perched on a small branch overhanging the river. Unbeknownst to us, a hippo swam *under* our canoe. With a frightening WHOOSH, it surfaced right beside us! I learned that I could take a picture and urinate at the same time.

The bow of my puny canoe gently comes to rest by a magnificent bull elephant on an island. Zimbabwe.

A storied word of Africa dramatically depicted on the leg bone of an elephant. Zimbabwe.

My minimal tent on the south bank of the Zambezi River, under a sausage tree and adjacent to a hippo trail, rates as one of my favorite spots in the whole of Africa . . . indeed, in the world. Zimbabwe.

Anticipation, excitement, and a sense of adventure always surged through me whenever I saw the camp staff carrying canoes down to the river. Zimbabwe.

Canoeing down the legendary Zambezi River is so carefree, so tranquil, so serene—

—until a hippo swims <u>under</u> your canoe . . .

. . . and then charges past you! Zimbabwe.

After the adrenalin rush from a hippo, an elephant is a welcome relief. Zimbabwe.

It was such fun to surprise my group with tables and camp stools . . .

. . . set on a sand bar in the river for an elaborate picnic lunch . . .

. . . at the best restaurant on the Zambezi! Zimbabwe.

When canoeing you learn to use binoculars and not spill your beer. Zimbabwe.

Preparing to overnight on "Survival Island," the most exclusive address on the Zambezi. Zimbabwe.

No tents, just canoe paddles in the sand with mosquito nets draped over our sleeping bags. Zimbabwe.

Lanterns were doused so we could enjoy the full impact of our "million-star hotel." Zimbabwe.

At first light, I was ready and eager for another day on the river. Zimbabwe.

This is the life! Hot tea at sunrise, even on Survival Island. Zimbabwe.

Now and then we would do a "Zambezi Legover," where we would each put a leg over into the adjacent canoe to form a unified flotilla . . . and let the rest of the world go by. Zimbabwe.

Would You Go on Safari with *This* Man?
Who the Cowabunga IS Gary Clarke?

I have been told that I do not fit the image of a "Safari Guide." You know: movie star handsome, full head of hair, clean shaven, flat belly, dashing and athletic, proper decorum. Nope, that's not me.

But I am content as I am. If you can't laugh at yourself . . . *who-can-you-laugh-at*? Besides, I don't take myself seriously since no one else seems to. Furthermore, it is difficult to be pompous on safari when you have to relieve yourself in the bush with a baboon looking on.

Image or not, leading safaris was a dream come true for me. It combined being a guide, a teacher, a protector, and even somewhat of a parent. As they say, "It's a tough job, but somebody's got to do it."

One of the great things about Africa is that you *can* be yourself, and you can really "let your hair down" assuming you have hair to let down. Even if you don't, you can enjoy yourself in an uninhibited way and be accepted by the Africans. In all of my time in Africa, never once did I hear someone say, "Oh, why-don't-you-grow-up?"

My zany antics and playful sense of humor have earned me a few nicknames. In East Africa, my Kiswahili name is *Mzee Shetani*, which translates to "Old Devil Man" because of my propensity for practical jokes. In Southern Africa, particularly the Zambezi Valley, I'm known as the "Old Dagga Boy" after an old, cantankerous male Cape buffalo. He is kicked out of the herd, is losing all of his hair (but *not* past his prime), and wallows in the mud (or dagga), which I have done on occasion. Of course, they simply call me "Cowabunga" all over Africa.

You may wonder about the "banana head" photo. It was on my first venture into Uganda. As we drove through the countryside, we saw numerous slim, erect women carrying huge stalks of green bananas (weighing sixty pounds or more) on their heads. At a bustling market I asked if I might have my photo taken with a stalk of green bananas on *my* head; they agreed. Struggle as I might, I just could not lift the stalk! The women burst into laughter. Then one put a small bunch of yellow bananas on my head and said, "Here, Cowabunga; for your picture!"

I've been called many names in Africa, but "banana head" is by far one of the nicest. Uganda.

You are always welcome to visit me at Main Camp in the Fairlawn Plaza Shopping Center in Topeka, Kansas, and take a ride in my Jeep, the Blue Dung Beetle, complete with Maasai cow bells. Some who meet me for the first time at Main Camp get the impression I am a competent and sensible Safari Leader. HA! Once on Safari, they learn otherwise . . . . Kansas, USA.

In Africa I am frequently lost. Tanzania.

I am rather inept when it comes to repairing a vehicle (that water was COLD!). Somewhere in Africa.

It seems I have a propensity to fraternize with giraffe. Kenya.

And I just can't take enough pictures. Kenya.

That's me in the bathtub at the old Ruckomechi Camp, as well as in that faded picture on the reed fence. As a result of that faded picture, I received letters from ladies around the world who told me I had watched them bathing. Zimbabwe.

The View from the Loo. Responding to Nature's call on a short drop in a bush camp—a perfect time to contemplate life and to formulate philosophies. Tanzania.

Your caption, please. Zambia.

*Despite the ashtrays, I do not smoke. Despite the empty bottles, I do not drink.
(Well, I might have a sundowner on a special occasion when I'm off duty.) Zimbabwe.*

Your caption, please. (Yes, that is elephant dung.)
Everywhere in Africa

Honoring my namesake with a set of horns from a defunct old male Cape buffalo. Zambia.

I am at my happiest when wallowing in the mud that has been churned over time by hundreds of elephant, buffalo and warthog. Zimbabwe.

I am delighted when members of my groups join me in this Cowabunga Safaris tradition (particularly those who vow, "You'll never get me in that mud!"). Zimbabwe.

A rare sighting of the Mythical God of the Zambezi River (a tough job, but . . .). Zimbabwe.

Between Sunlight and Thunder
Quintessential Expressions of Africa

How well I remember the high excitement and eager anticipation before my first safari. I was thirty-five years old and had been seemingly preparing for this milestone event all my life. I thought I knew what it would be like. I did not. My journey to Kenya and Tanzania in 1974 exceeded every expectation.

Evelyn Ames said it so well in ***A Glimpse of Eden***: *"Nothing can really prepare you for Africa: it is too full of extremes and contrasts, too immense—a spectrum of creation so much wider and more vivid than anywhere else that it seems to require a new set of senses, or the rediscovery of lost ones."*

To my surprise, the emotional impact of Africa was something I had never felt before—somewhere between sunlight and thunder. I felt things that I did not understand, I had feelings difficult to express. In the middle of the savannah, surrounded by a sea of grass, I felt like I was at the center of the universe. In the stillness of the night, with the profound mystery of darkness, I felt suspended in time and space. But always, in Africa, I felt at home, so natural and so fulfilled, with a sense of belonging. I felt as one with the rhythm and heartbeat of the earth. Whenever I would leave Africa I always felt a loss, as though a part of my being had remained behind, and I had to function much like a less-than-complete individual with my life out of balance.

While still on safari, Ernest Hemingway once remarked: "I'm so homesick for Africa, and I haven't even left yet."

How well I understand his sentiment.

At this stage in my life, even though my physical presence is no longer there, I feel serene in knowing that the ancient rhythms of Africa continue—between sunlight and thunder.

And now, dear reader, please adjust your book one-quarter turn for the full-frame horizontal images. Thank you.

Giraffe magically drift between sunlight and thunder over a savannah dreamscape. Only in Africa.

As Africa comes alive in the early morning mist, a lioness scouts for prey. Kenya.

Like an apparition, two bull elephant gradually become visible as they cross a dry lake bed. Kenya.

Roosting in the drowned trees of Lake Kariba, cormorants and darters complement the sunset. Zimbabwe.

To be on the Victoria Nile, to photograph a bull hippo against papyrus, is to know you are on Safari! Uganda.

Dusk in the African bush is a special time . . . as is dawn . . . and midnight . . . and . . . . Anytime in Africa.

What a remarkable experience to have this lioness be so accepting of my presence in her habitat. Kenya.

Portrait of the bull hippo that gently bumped our launch in the Kazinga Channel, Uganda.

A male great Kudu forms part of the fabric of his bush habitat. Botswana.

With increased lung capacity and long legs, the diurnal cheetah catches prey on the run. Tanzania.

As the prince of cats, powerfully built and adept at climbing, the nocturnal leopard hunts by stealth. Kenya.

Alert plains zebra in the Ngorongoro Crater cautiously observe a lion as it strolls in the distance. Tanzania.

Africa in silhouette. Kenya.

Long shadows of mother and baby giraffe from our balloon. Kenya.

Flying in a second balloon, I calculated the precise moment to partially block glare from the sun. Tanzania.

Sunlight and dust give birth to a phantom giraffe. Zimbabwe.

Your caption, please. Kenya.

232

Tension in the bush . . . impending storm and Cape buffalo. Rwanda.

Predator . . . prey . . . scavenger . . . the cycle of the bush. Kenya.

A fisherman on the South Luangwa River at dusk cautiously navigates among hippo and crocodile. Zambia.

In African folklore, the baobab tree was planted upside down with its roots exposed to the sky. Tanzania.

From a jolting Land Rover, my slow-film photo of a running cheetah in mid-air was so fortuitous! Tanzania.

Vibrant and robust in his semiarid habitat, this Grant's gazelle may be the finest specimen I've seen. Kenya.

A pair of olive baboon drink in a Rift Valley stream, with the female showing signs of estrus. Tanzania.

Twilight in the African bush creates such a spectacular afterglow that the lioness is just a bonus. Zimbabwe.

Marabou storks prepare to roost for the night. Kenya.

Adapted for aquatic life, the Nile crocodile has nostrils, eyes and ear slits along the top of its head. Zambia.

Zebra and wildebeest mingle among the yellow fever trees on the floor of the Ngorongoro Crater, Tanzania.

Your caption, please. Kenya.

Waterbuck seek shade under an acacia tree complete with the distinctive hanging nests of weaver birds. Kenya.

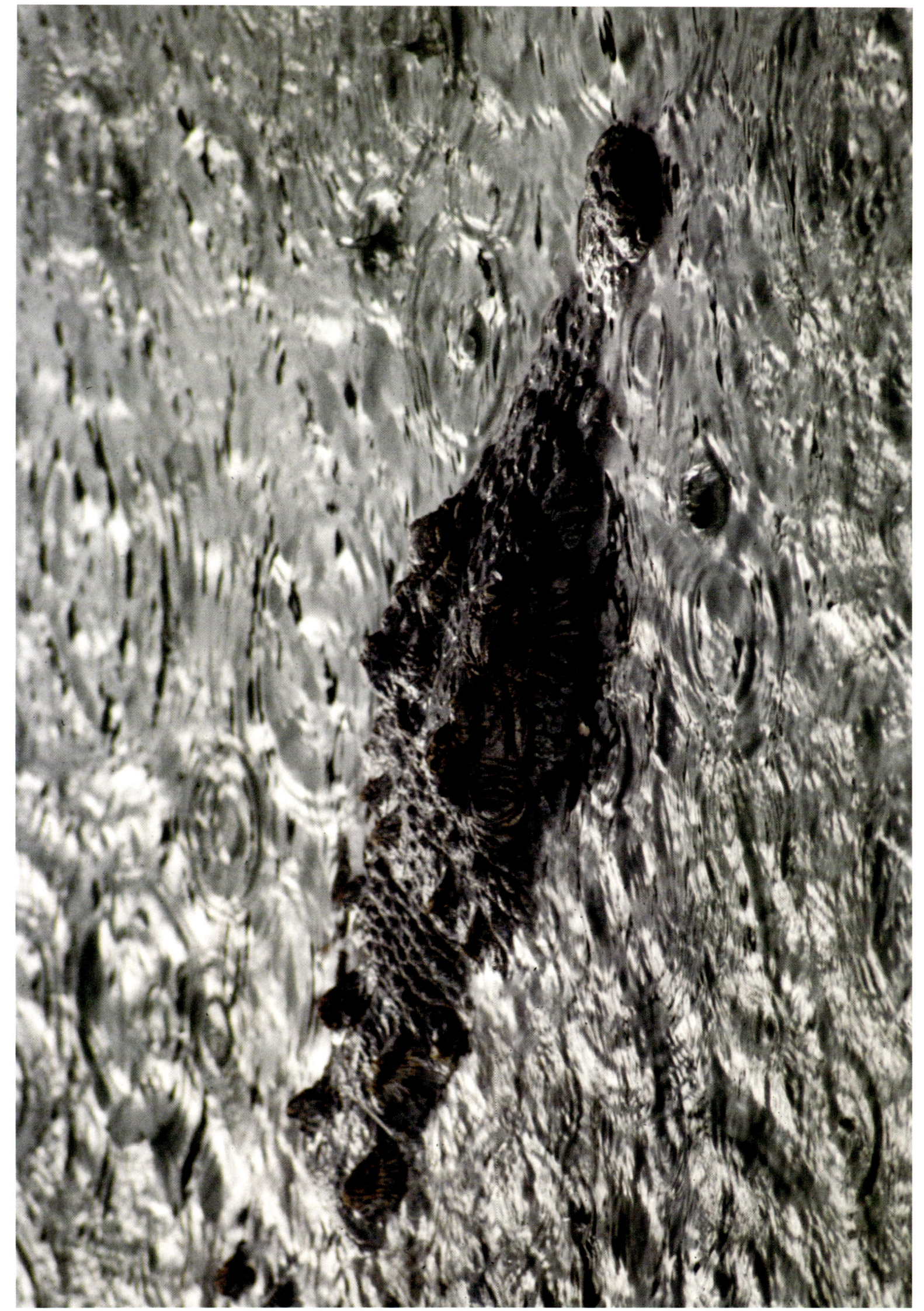

One of my favorite images! A crocodile blends with water textured by the pelting rain. South Africa.

These stately male lion, "Monarchs of the Mara," are brothers and share a pride. Kenya.

In the heat of midday a small acacia tree provides beneficial shade for a Grevy's zebra stallion. Kenya.

A Cape buffalo skull by my tent along the Zambezi symbolizes Africa as my final resting place. Zimbabwe.

My photo from a boat among drowned trees in Lake Kariba. No tricks. True image. Real Africa. Zimbabwe.

Such a privilege to be so close to an elephant in Africa that I can see the "sleep-gunk" in his eye! Tanzania.

The black rhino has a hooked lip for browsing, while the white rhino has a flat mouth for grazing. Tanzania.

Unlike a leopard, the cheetah has "tear marks" on the face and solid spots rather than rosettes. South Africa.

The lesser known king cheetah has a mane, "stripes" on the back, and blotches on legs and flanks. South Africa.

The drinking posture of a giraffe makes it vulnerable to predators. Namibia.

Giraffe on a flooded savannah. Kenya.

256

Nature creates dramatic and ever-changing masterpieces in the African sky. Oh, how I miss Africa. Kenya.

The zebra on the right heard my camera click and looked. Did you notice the baby? Namibia.

After patrolling his territory, a male leopard rests and surveys. South Africa.

Reflections at twilight. Zimbabwe.

Well, gentle reader, the cheetah is bored....

. . . and the hippo are asleep. So, it must be . . . .

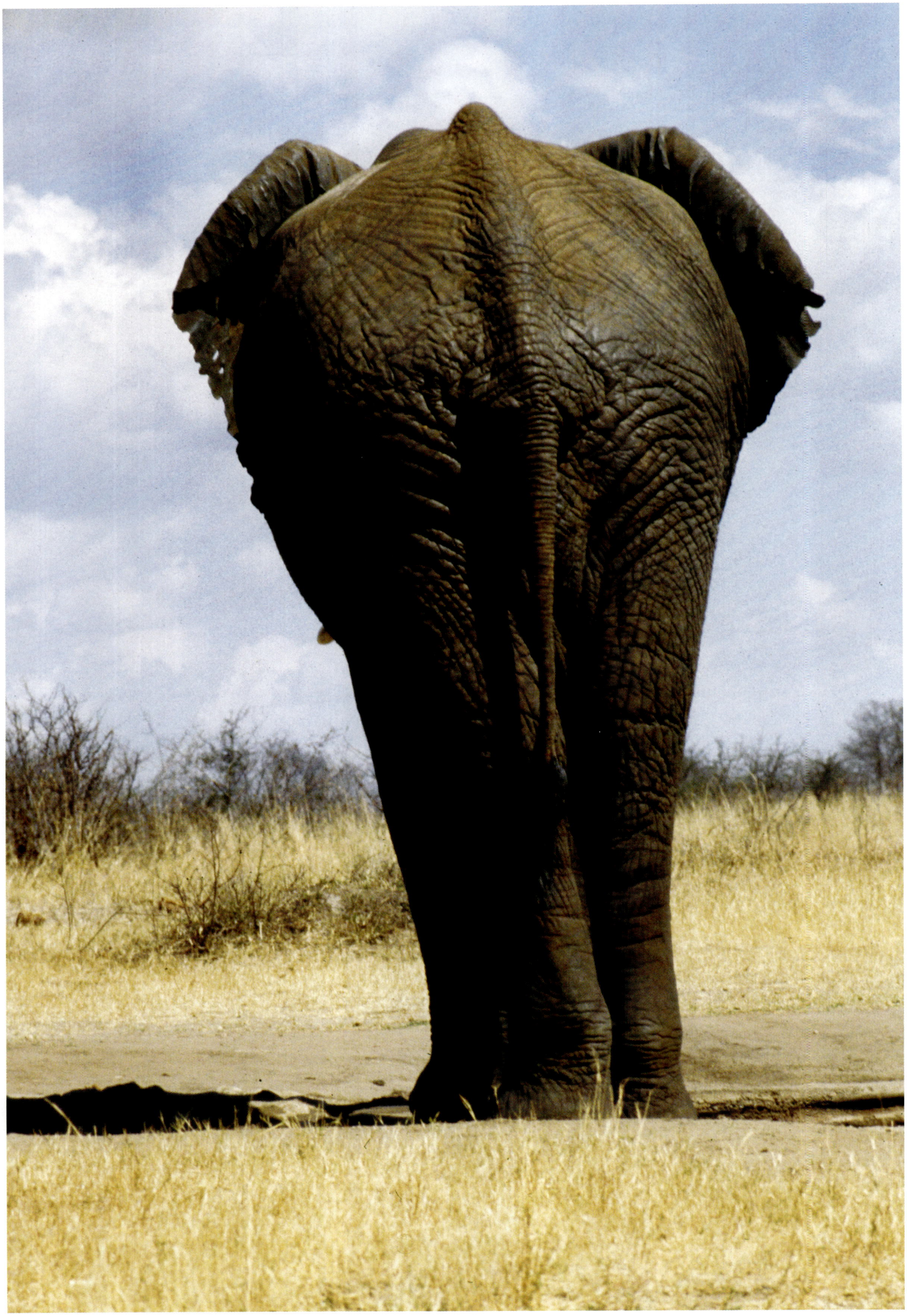

Africa under a rainbow.

Visions of Africa

When I started this project, the intent was simple: to share with you the joy of the safari experience and what Africa means to me. Now, however, I realize that the resulting book is so much more than I expected.

It is a window into my heart.

In merely reviewing my safari photographs and journals, compiled over three decades, little did I dream how vividly I would relive so many of the most treasured moments of my life. Little did I dream that these memories of Africa would stir my very soul.

I *miss* Africa.

The safari gods smiled on me, and I acknowledge that fact with humble gratitude. In the year 2006, I completed safari number 140. Was that my last campfire? I would hope not, but it seems unlikely I shall ever be able to return.

I *crave* Africa.

Still, it is gratifying that so many of my longtime Cowabunga Safaris alumni continually urge me to lead "just one more grand safari." They offer such enticements as, "We'll do all the work," and "we just want you along for your bad puns and corny jokes."

I *yearn* for Africa.

Just as heartwarming are the regular pleas to return to Africa from my friends *in* Africa. The gamut is incredible, including some Maasai in Tanzania who beseech: "Cowabunga, when are you coming home? We have built a dung covered house for you; we have cows for you; we have wives for you; Cowabunga, when are you coming?"

And there is the standing invitation, from my trustworthy guides on the Zambezi river, to do one last safari for "old-times' sake"—canoeing, mud wallowing, and simply being surrounded by wildlife.

I *ache* for Africa.

Visions of Africa are forever with me: the smoke and thunder of Victoria Falls; the green immensity of the Serengeti; the intrigue and romance of Timbuktu; the soaring, cloud-wreathed volcano that is Kilimanjaro; the excitement and grandeur of the Great Rift Valley; the savage sparkle of the Zambezi.

Damn! I miss Africa . . .

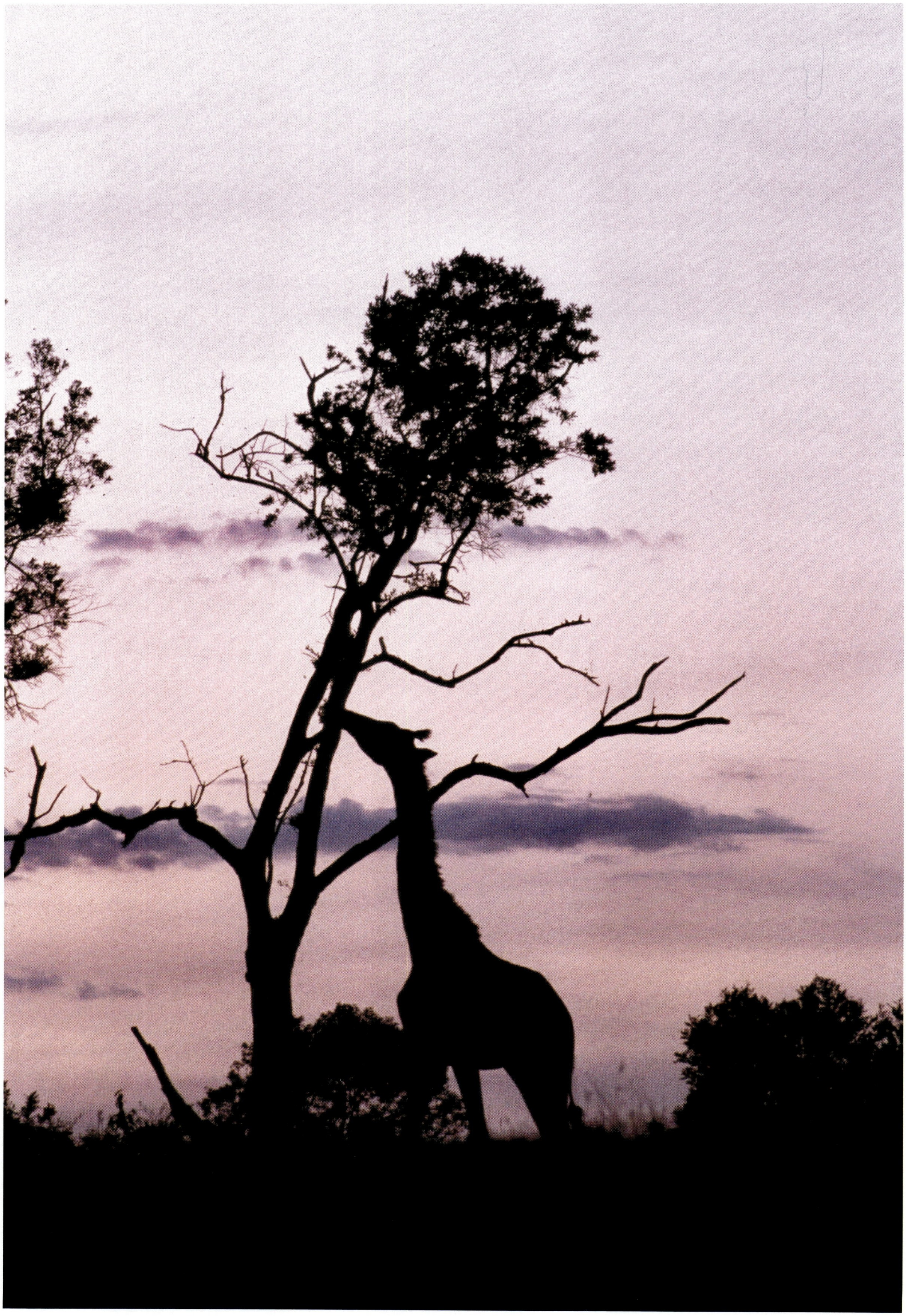

A Safari Prayer

I have eyes
 to see the glorious sunset . . . and the enchanting moonrise

I have ears
 to hear the melodious birdsong . . . and the whispering river

I have a nose
 to smell the dust, the dung . . . and the smoke of the campfire

I have a tongue
 to taste the cool water . . . and the warm beer

I have skin
 to feel the hot sun . . . and the gentle breeze

I have hands
 to touch the magnificent baobab . . . and the elegant acacia tree

I have feet
 to follow the tracks of life on trails in the bush

I have a spirit
 to be one with nature:
  hippo and hyena
   lion and crocodile
    warthog and elephant

I have friends
 with whom to share these wonders

I have family
 whose love and understanding sustain and inspire me

Truly I am blessed.

—Gary K. Clarke
Whilst on Safari

Asante Sana/Ngiyabonga Kakhulu

So many people helped with this book that I should say "thank you" in an array of African languages, not merely Kiswahili and Zulu as per the heading. Just as a Safari is a team effort, so was the production of this book—and what a team! My images on film were scanned and digitized by Joe Sutcliffe, who also did the initial computer layout of the photos and captions from my basic mock-up. Mary Napier took my rough draft typescript and coordinated it with the photographic images for the final layout and design. As part of the process Randy Austin applied his editorial and wordsmithing skills and helped me "chase the welds." Sherry Best led the technical effort, Rod Furgason lent his artistic talent, and Lloyd Zimmer (my bookman in Topeka) assisted greatly with the various facets of publishing a limited edition book.

Many people reviewed all or part of my draft manuscript, including: Randy Austin, Sherry Best, Lloyd Zimmer, Dr. Schuyler Jones, CBE, Brian Hesse, PhD, James G. Doherty, Loretta Caravette, Ken Kawata, Paul Breese, Debra Foster, Mary Ellen Walter, Robert Wagner, Mark Rosenthal, Mary A. Hall, Conrad & Judy Froehlich, Jacque Borgeson, Tim Degginger, Neta Jeffus, Joe Sutcliffe, Rod Furgason, Mary Napier, Ken Redman, Rod & Mary Jane Bowen, Ken & Jane Yocum, Phil Lange, Ron Kaufman, Mark & Sharon Boranyak, Mickey Ollson, Dick Knoll, DeWitt Harkness, Kathy Groesbeck, Steve Taylor, Jim Bertoncin, Cheryl & John McAuley, Steve & Kathy Clarke, Evie Green, Kim Van Aswegen. I am deeply grateful to all of them.

I have received widespread encouragement and spiritual support from all of the above as well as: Drs. Ken & Margie Blanchard, Carlos & Sharon Arbelaez, Dorothy Harvey, Debbie Bryant, David Livingstone (a living descendant of the original), John Ngomo, Garth Thompson, James Varden, the Cummings family, Nick Greaves, Max and Carol Yoho, Jack Hanna, Rick Prebeg, Doug & Irene Hommert, Ed Carmona, the Mark Morris, Jr. family, Phil Grecian, Nathan Ham, Susan & Gary Chan, the staff of Topeka and Shawnee County Public Library, my Main Camp neighbors Fairlawn Plaza Style Center and Reuter's Inc., Marshall & Katrina Clark, Ray Miller, Joe & Rita Sutcliffe, Marcia Coder & Dale Schneider, Rod & Jan Furgason, the Jim Bryan family, Blenda Blankenship, Naomi Nibbelink, Alice Johnston, Bob & Marilyn Johnson, Betty Bulkley, Tom Welch, Bob Wheeler, Gary Lee, Bill Dennler, Dave Zucconi, Cynthia & Charlie Robinson, Marcy Love, Kent & Janet McKinney, Joan Obits, Suzanne Mudget, Joe Gates, Sue Drais, Margie Linck, Jackie McQueary, Don & Carol Jackson, Nancy Murphy, Bob & Nancy Brenton, Betty Hoffer, Marion Brenton, JoAnn Myers, Fritzie Walker, Helen Bondurant, Phil & Collette Coolidge, Mike & Kathy McCrite, the Mike Basel family, Vera Pearce, Jim & Mary Beth Schroff, Phil & Marsha Oliver, Susan Wimmer, Jim Ellis, Mike and Shari Larue, Roger and Lanette Scurlock, Ron and Linda Kaufman, Dick Houston, Dennis Baranski, *plus* all of my valued friends in Africa, as well as Mzee and Mzungu Mrefu. I am humbled by everyone's continuous support and appreciative of their friendship.

Some of the images in the book were first seen as part of the exhibition "Gary Clarke's Africa" in the then Gallery of Fine Arts at the Topeka and Shawnee County Public Library; my appreciation to the Library and to Larry Peters, former gallery director. Special thanks as well to the many staff over the years at Wolfe's Camera Shops, Inc., in Topeka for conscientiously handling countless rolls of my irreplaceable film after *each* Safari, and for serving as a resource on all things photographic. With the exception of the photos that include me, I took all of the photographs (save one). A most sincere *Asante* to the other photographers: your pictures afford a more complete view of the total Cowabunga Safaris experience.

Far beyond this book, my family has long supported my passion for Africa and, in doing so, they have shown their love for Africa as well. To them I express my deep love and gratitude.

Other Notions of Gary Clarke's
AFRICA
by Rod Furgason
Cowabunga Safaris Alumnus

"Must be another book by Gary Clarke."

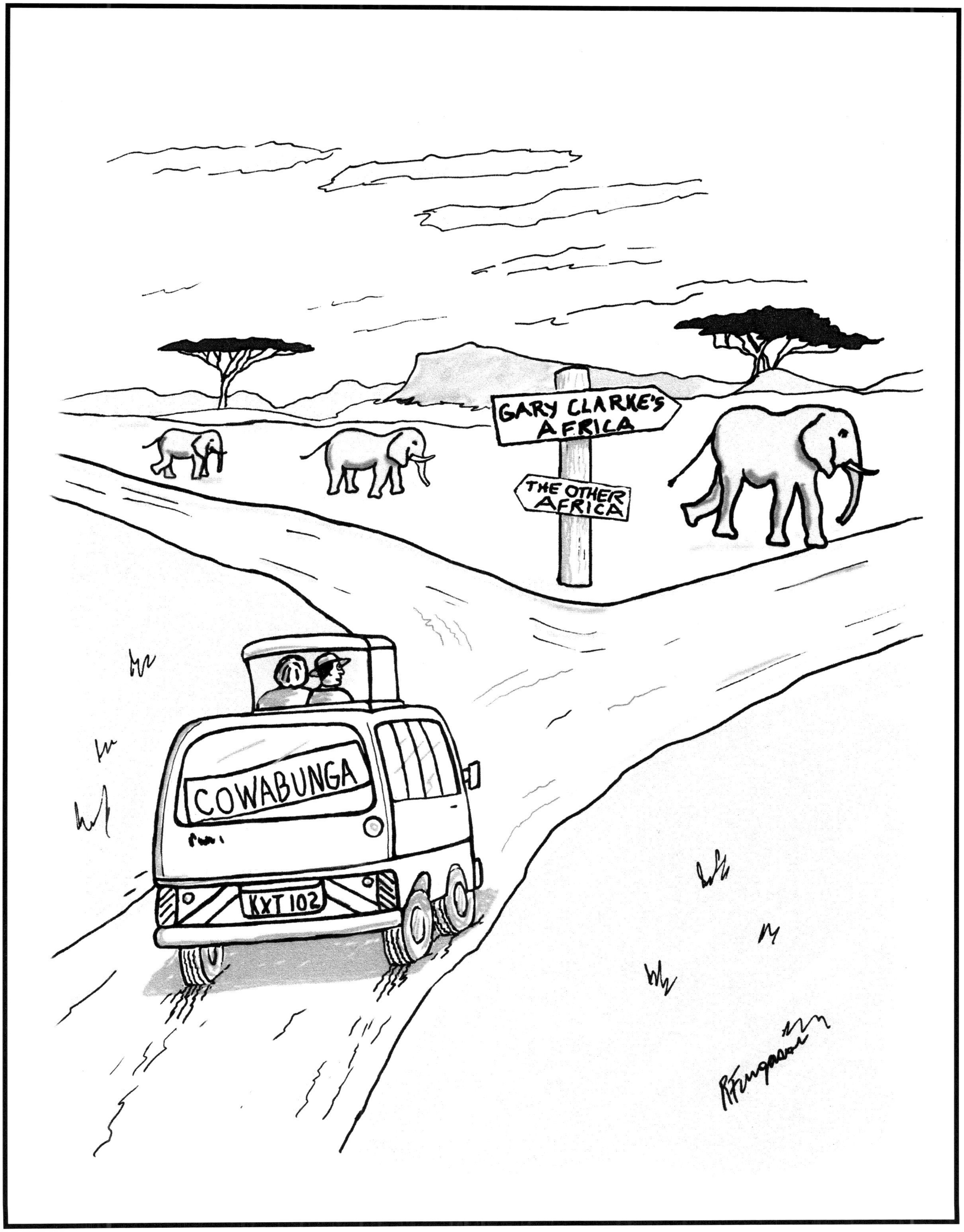
GARY CLARKE'S AFRICA
THE OTHER AFRICA
COWABUNGA
KXT 102

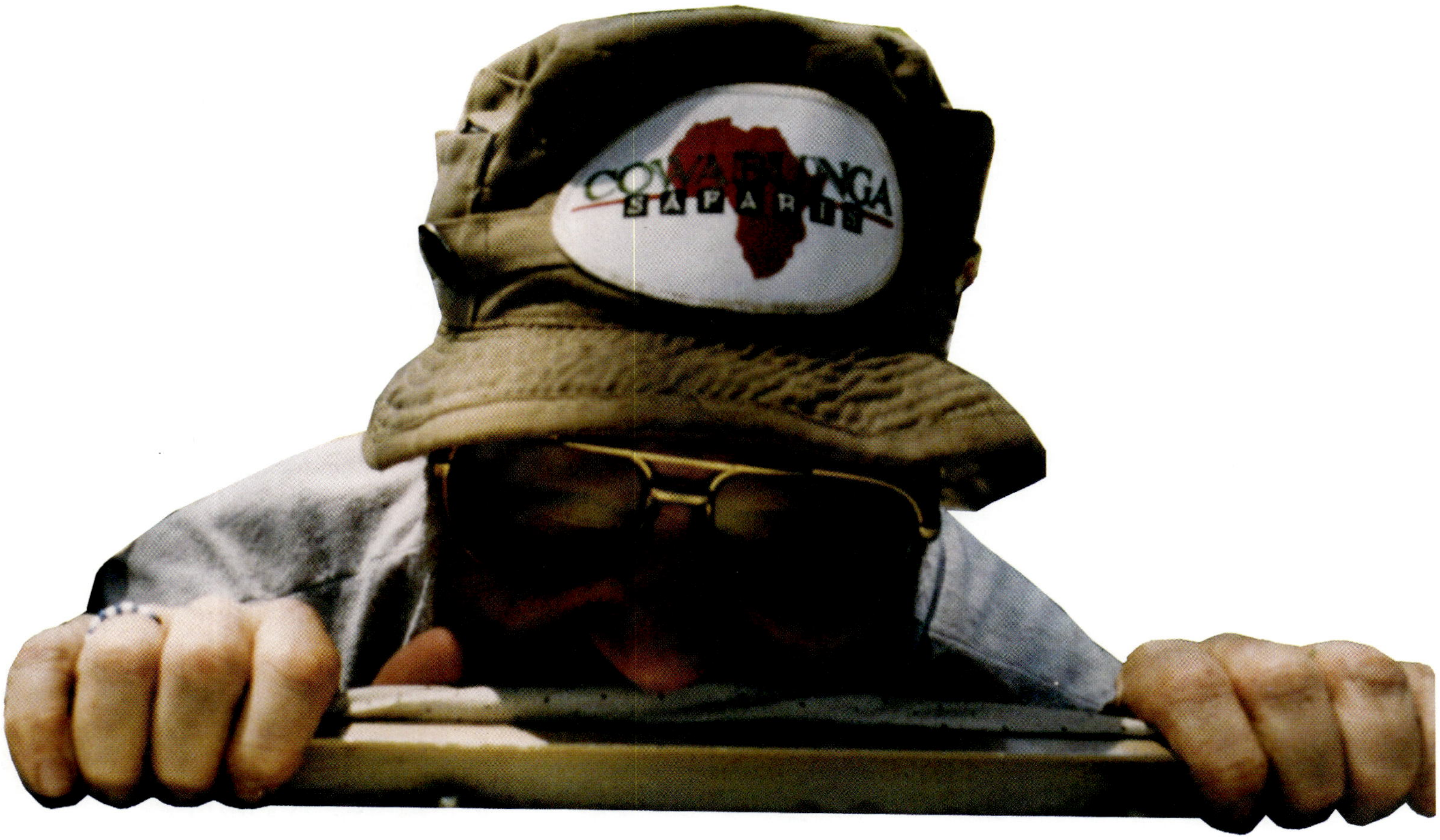

Osa Johnson's 1941 book Four Years in Paradise is an account of the Johnsons' famed 1924-1927 stay at the mystical Lake Paradise in northern Kenya. This book had a distinctive giraffe-patterned cover to match the zebra-striped cover of I Married Adventure. The covers of these books were inspired by the paint schemes of Martin and Osa's Sikorsky amphibious planes, her "Osa's Ark" zebra-striped S-38 and his "Spirit of Africa and Borneo" giraffe-spotted S-39.